T0378512

Holocaust Atrocities
NAZI DEATH CAMPS

Don Nardo

San Diego, CA

About the Author

In addition to his award-winning books about the ancient world, historian Don Nardo has written extensively about World War II, including studies of the Pacific campaigns against Japan, the rise and fall of Nazi Germany, and a well-reviewed biography of Adolf Hitler. Nardo, who also composes and arranges orchestral music, lives with his wife, Christine, in Massachusetts.

Picture Credits:

Cover: Everett Collection/Shutterstock.com
 6: Shawshots/Alamy Stock Photo
10: Maury Aaseng
12: Joel Bellviure/Mediadrumworld/ZUMA Press/
    Newscom
15: Buyenlarge Archive/UIG/Bridgeman Images
20: Everett Collection/Shutterstock.com
22: World History Archive/Alamy Stock Photo
24: Serhii Khomiak/Shutterstock.com

30: CBW/Alamy Stock Photo
33: Rafel/Shutterstock.com
34: Pictures from History/Newscom
39: Keystone Press/Alamy Stock Photo
43: akg-images/Newscom
45: Matytsin Valery/ZUMA Press/Newscom
49: Photoshot/Newscom
51: Ian Clarke/Alamy Stock Photo
55: Shanae Ennis-Malhado/Shutterstock.com

LIBRARY OF CONGRESS CATALOGING-IN-PUBLICATION DATA

Names: Nardo, Don, 1947- author.
Title: Holocaust atrocities : Nazi death camps / by Don Nardo.
Description: San Diego, CA : ReferencePoint Press, 2025. | Includes
   bibliographical references and index.
Identifiers: LCCN 2024001265 (print) | LCCN 2024001266 (ebook) | ISBN
   9781678208004 (library binding) | ISBN 9781678208011 (ebook)
Subjects: LCSH: Nazi concentration camps--Europe--Juvenile literature. |
   Holocaust, Jewish (1939-1945)--Juvenile literature.
Classification: LCC D805.A2 N37 2025 (print) | LCC D805.A2 (ebook) | DDC
   365/.450943--dc23/eng/20240122
LC record available at https://lccn.loc.gov/2024001265
LC ebook record available at https://lccn.loc.gov/2024001266

A Place of Life and Death

Millions of people died in or near the extermination camps run by the German Nazis in Poland during World War II. Day in and day out, Jews and others marked for death by the Nazis were killed by poison gas, firing squads, or slow starvation and overwork. Typically, their remains were either buried or burned in large ovens called crematoria. At the most notorious death camp, Auschwitz, an estimated 1.1 million people were systematically murdered during the war.

A Spark of Life

Amid these horrors—in the face of so many gruesome deaths—remarkably, the spark of life was not completely extinguished. "It's strange to think of the camp as a place of life as well [as death],"[1] says journalist Erin Blakemore. Yet it was. Many new lives came into the world at Auschwitz, thanks to the tireless work of a Polish midwife named Stanislawa Leszczyńska. Leszczyńska was interned at Auschwitz in 1943 because of her family's efforts to help Jews trapped by the Nazis in the Polish ghetto of Lodz. In the two years of her internment, she delivered some three thousand babies—the children of prisoners who were pregnant when they entered the camp.

Most women who arrived at Auschwitz pregnant were immediately sent to their deaths. And the Nazis made it clear that many of the infants Leszczyńska brought into the world would be promptly killed at birth. Even so, the camp officers allowed her to do this work.

Leszczyńska soon learned why she was allowed to bring these babies into the world. The Nazis, it turns out, were watching for babies born with fair hair and blue eyes, traits they deemed superior. Some of those babies were taken from their mothers and given to adoption agencies, which in turn placed the infants with German parents who were unable to have their own children.

In spite of the grim reality in the camp, Leszczyńska forged ahead, hoping to save at least some of the infants and to relieve the suffering of some of their mothers. Working under horrendous conditions, she persevered and took pride in her work. "Contrary to all expectations and in spite of the extremely inauspicious conditions," she said after the war, "all the babies born in the concentration camp were born alive and looked healthy at birth. Nature defied hatred and extermination and stubbornly fought for her rights, drawing on an unknown reserve of vitality."[2]

> "[All those children I delivered at Auschwitz] were born alive and looked healthy at birth."[2]
>
> —Auschwitz inmate and midwife Stanislawa Leszczyńska

According to medical historians Susan Benedict and Linda Shields, most of the three thousand infants Leszczyńska birthed were murdered soon after delivery, and about five hundred of them were secretly placed with families. But about thirty were still alive in the camp when it was liberated at the war's end. One of the mothers, Maria Saloman, who survived along with her newborn, later reminisced, "My Liz owes her life to Stanislawa Leszczyńska. I cannot think of her without tears coming to my eyes."[3]

The Chief Symbol of a Despicable Regime

The death camps that the Nazis erected in Poland, along with dozens of concentration camps throughout Europe, were created on the orders of Adolf Hitler. Hitler rose to power in Germany in 1933. He initiated World War II in September 1939 with the invasion of Poland. His two chief aims were to conquer all of

This 1945 photo shows survivors of Auschwitz on the day of their liberation. While there were many horrors at the extermination camps, the spark of life was not completely extinguished.

Europe and to exterminate anyone who opposed him or whom he deemed inferior. The camps provided him with a way to fulfill that second goal by controlling, dehumanizing, and ultimately murdering millions of people.

Hitler's first goal, European conquest, ultimately failed. In 1945 his regime—the Third Reich—catastrophically collapsed. But his twisted aim of ridding Europe of Jews and other people whom Hitler believed were unfit to live nearly succeeded. Of the more than 50 million people who died in the war, at least 11 million were murdered outright. Among those victims were some 6 million Jews, or about 60 percent of Europe's Jewish population. The systematic, state-sponsored killing of Jews by the Nazis, part of a plan to eliminate all Jews from Europe, has come to be known as the Holocaust. Among the millions of other victims of Hitler's murderous campaign were the Roma (then more widely known as Gypsies), Communists, gay people, disabled individuals, prisoners of war, and ordinary civilians in many villages in and around Poland.

Poland turned out to be the epicenter of the mass murders perpetrated by the Nazis during the war. Under Hitler's orders, Nazi henchmen slaughtered huge numbers of people in that region, often by mowing them down with machine guns. Yet the largest number of the victims dispatched in and around Poland were those gassed and starved to death in the region's death camps, which became a chief symbol of the corrupt and brutal Nazi regime. As University of London scholar Nikolaus Wachsmann points out, those camps "embodied the spirit of Naziism like no other institution in the Third Reich." They were the main "sites of lawless terror, where some of the most radical features of Nazi rule were born and refined."[4] It is not surprising, therefore, that the Nazis' camps are still, and likely always will be, recorded among history's worst examples of human cruelty and brutality.

> "[The death camps were Germany's main] sites of lawless terror, where some of the most radical features of Nazi rule were born."[4]
>
> —University of London historian Nikolaus Wachsmann

CHAPTER ONE

Rise of the Nazi Death Camps

Interviewed in 1945, shortly after the close of World War II, Jozef Pogorzelski, a Polish railway worker, testified about the Nazi facilities near the village of Treblinka in northeastern Poland. As late as July 1942, he and his fellow workers thought there was only a labor camp there for prisoners of war. But later that month Pogorzelski and his colleagues learned they had been mistaken. It was then that the first trains carrying large numbers of European civilians arrived. "There was a horrible smell of dead bodies wafting to the station," Pogorzelski said. "And it was then that we all realized that there was another camp in Treblinka, next to the labour camp—an extermination camp."[5]

Pogorzelski and his coworkers reasoned that a death camp existed just beyond the Treblinka labor camp based on their observations of the simple logistics of the situation. Each week several trains, each heavily loaded with people, left the main railway line and went down a spur, or separate track, that led to the rear of the labor camp. A railway official whom Pogorzelski knew well told him that one of those transports held at least ten thousand people. Moreover, the official said, "there were a lot of corpses in the wagons."[6] In addition, when the trains came back out onto the main line, they were always empty. These facts, coupled with the smell of death that hung over the area, were enough for Pogorzelski and the others to piece together what was happening.

A Vast Network of Camps

Although these Polish railway workers were right in their suspicion that a concentration camp where people were murdered existed at Treblinka, they had no inkling that that facility was part of a growing network of similar camps. The exact number remains unknown, but historians estimate there may have been around one thousand scattered across Germany and several nearby nations conquered by the Nazis. All were what people today call concentration camps. Each housed people against their will, and the Nazis committed mass murders in varying numbers in all of them. But their specific purposes and uses by the Nazis varied somewhat.

Some were designated *labor* camps, for instance, although the inmates in all the concentration camps performed work on a daily basis. The jobs the prisoners did were diverse—such as making synthetic rubber, synthetic oil, explosives, and other materials to support the German war effort. Similar jobs were done by inmates in another type of Nazi camp reserved mainly for prisoners of war—mostly British, French, Polish, Soviet, and other captured enemy soldiers. There were also so-called *transit* camps, where prisoners stayed temporarily on their way to other camps. No matter how the camps were designated, they all featured living conditions that were unsanitary and inhumane. And when a prisoner could no longer be effectively exploited, he or she was summarily murdered.

Within the vast Nazi camp network were six additional, specialized camps. These were the extermination camps, sometimes called death camps. All were erected in Poland, which had been overrun by Germany in 1939. The death camps were named for towns they were in or near: Chelmno, Belzec, Sobibor, Treblinka, Majdanek, and Auschwitz-Birkenau (or Auschwitz). They were constructed primarily for killing as many people as possible in the shortest time span. The unfortunate inmates were typically described as "undesirables" or "inferior" in the Nazi ideology promoted by Adolf Hitler. Included in these groups were Jews, Communists, Gypsies, gay people, people with disabilities, and others.

Ghettos, Camps, and Killing Centers, 1942

Note: dotted lines show present-day borders

Why the Nazis Targeted Jews

Of these doomed individuals, none were more despised by Hitler and his Nazi followers than the Jews. This deep-seated hatred derived primarily from Hitler's experiences during and after World War I. He had served as a low-level army infantryman in that massive conflict. When his nation lost the war, he became bitter and at times depressed. Although upset about losing the war, many Germans did their best to get on with their lives. But Hitler's dismay and sense of loss remained acute, and he soothed himself by believing and spreading falsehoods about who was responsible for Germany's defeat. Rather than accepting that the defeat lay with the nation's political and military leaders, Hitler blamed various groups within Germany. Among them were Communists, liberal politicians, bankers, and especially Jews. These groups, he claimed, had betrayed the country. And Hitler planned to make them pay.

Aside from scapegoating these groups, Hitler spoke in glowing terms of the rise once again of the German people. Deeply frustrated by their country's defeat and the continuing hardships of that loss, the people gravitated to Hitler's pronouncements of a more hopeful and powerful future. This was the opening Hitler needed. In 1919 he joined a tiny, obscure sociopolitical group, the German Workers' Party. Largely because he was an extraordinarily effective public speaker, the party grew swiftly. By 1925, now called the National Socialist Party, or Nazi Party, it boasted over fifty-five thousand members. Thereafter, it continued to expand, in part because of the effective use of fear tactics. To enforce his will, Hitler formed a small army of brutal street thugs—the SS (*Schutzstaffel*, or "defense corps"). They regularly beat, harassed, and threatened not only Jews but anyone who questioned or opposed the Nazis.

The anti-Jewish, antidemocratic speeches and tactics Hitler and his cronies employed proved successful over time. In January 1933 he was able to take control of Germany's government and then quickly pushed through several new laws that granted him dictatorial powers. Germany was now a police state in which Jews and others Hitler targeted were branded as dishonest and corrupt. Although Germany had a large and well-established Jewish community, Hitler proclaimed the Jews as inferior to "true Germans," whom the Nazis claimed made up a superior racial group—the Aryans.

Typical of this dangerous propaganda was a speech delivered in late 1933 by the director of a leading German women's organization. She advocated that Jews be punished rather than pitied for what she described as their natural inadequacies. The Jew, she said, was "a subtle poison since he destroys what is necessary to our life. If we are to be healed as a people [and] conquer a place in the world that is our due, then we must free ourselves ruthlessly from that parasite."[7]

Only a few short years after these words were spoken, the official method the Nazis developed to "free themselves" from the Jews was to confine them in concentration camps. And in short order, after the start of World War II, confinement was abandoned in favor of outright extermination. SS leader Heinrich Himmler, who was given overall charge of the death camps, repeatedly said that

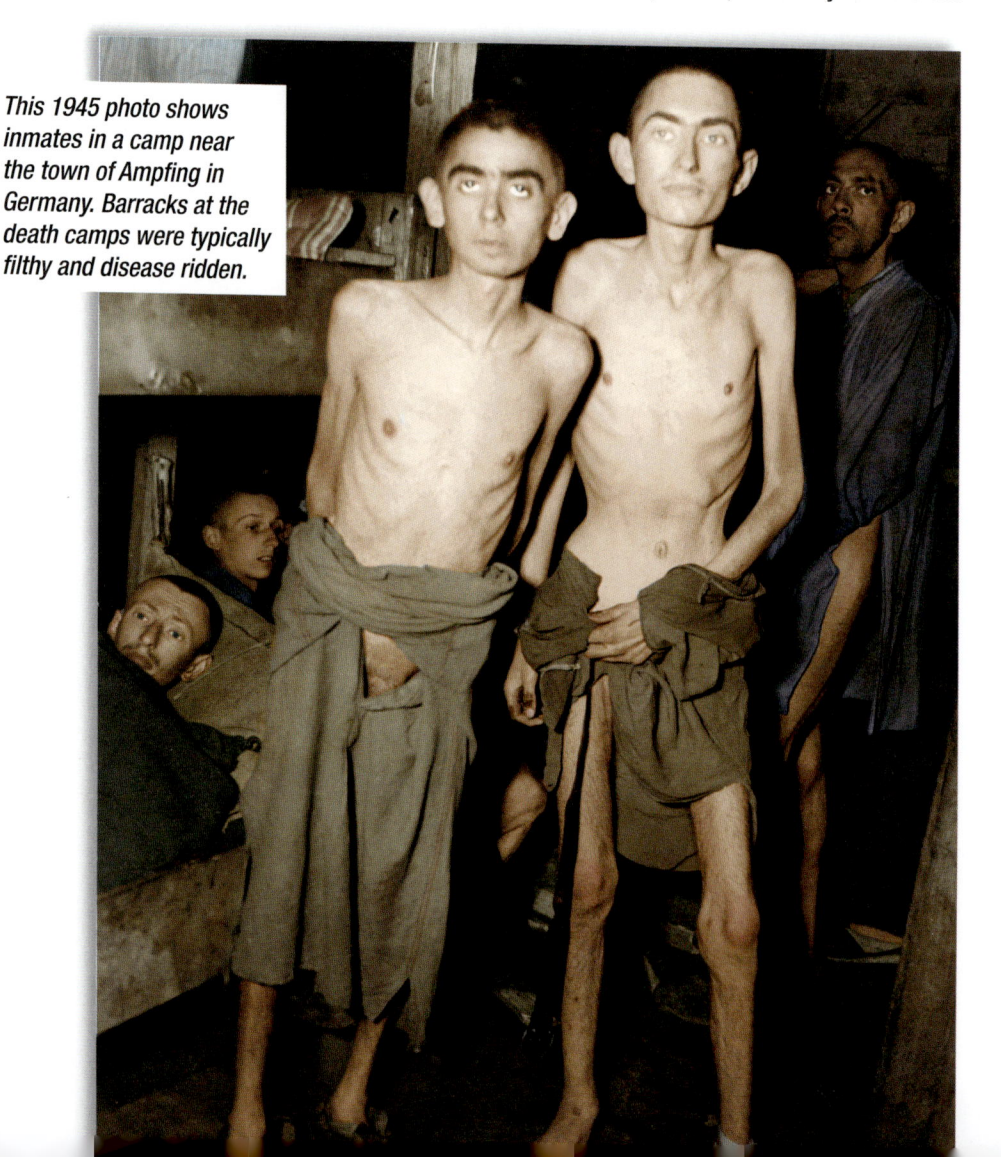

This 1945 photo shows inmates in a camp near the town of Ampfing in Germany. Barracks at the death camps were typically filthy and disease ridden.

The Man with the Iron Heart

Reinhard Heydrich was one of the most feared Nazis in the Third Reich. As head of the Gestapo, Germany's secret police, Heydrich was responsible for rounding up Jews and consigning them to ghettos and concentration camps. His most important job, however, was to plan and enact the Final Solution, the mass murder of Europe's Jews. To that end, Heydrich organized the death squads—the *Einsatzgruppen*—that killed thousands of Jews in mass shootings. He also helped plan the layout and mass murder apparatus of the death camps before he was assassinated by Czech freedom fighters in May 1942. Heydrich was so cruel to people the Nazis opposed that his enemies gave him the unflattering nicknames of the Hangman and the Young Evil God of Death. Recognizing the man's cold, unsympathetic nature, Hitler himself called him the Man with the Iron Heart.

Jewish children were particularly threatening. If they were allowed to survive, he warned, they would "grow up to wreak vengeance on our children and grandchildren." Hence, he said, true Germans must "make these people [the Jews] disappear from the face of the earth."[8]

A Model for the Death Camps

Physically speaking, the six extermination camps that Himmler oversaw resembled the labor concentration camp at Dachau, situated about 10 miles (16.1 km) northwest of the German city of Munich. Although not intended to be a death camp, more than any other single facility, it acted as a model for the general layout of Sobibor, Auschwitz, and other death camps.

First opening in March 1933, Dachau was divided into two main sections. One consisted primarily of inmates' living facilities, including thirty-two long, rectangular barracks, where they slept in bunks stacked in three or more levels. The interiors of these structures were extremely drab, dismal, and uncomfortable. Meanwhile, support buildings near the barracks housed a kitchen, a laundry, and various workshops.

The other principal section of Dachau contained the sinister means of controlling and disposing of the inmates. This included places where they were punished and tortured, buildings where they were gassed to death, and pits where their bodies were either buried or burned. The camp was fully surrounded by a tall, sturdy barbed-wire fence that was electrified with enough voltage to stun or kill anyone who touched it.

Dachau was run by a commandant. The daily business of the camp was overseen by guards. Both commandant and guards were most often members of the SS. The SS served as the elite guard of the Nazi regime. Its primary duty was to remove and kill all political and so-called racial enemies of the Third Reich. In particular, the SS oversaw the massacre of Europe's Jewish population.

How to Transport Victims Cost-Effectively?

To achieve this goal, the Nazis began rounding up all those people slated for death. During 1938 to 1941, Jews and other people seen as undesirable were forced into ghettos—small sections of cities that could be easily cordoned off so that no one could enter or leave without permission. The object was to trap, isolate, guard, and control the Jews living in a given region.

> "[The Final Solution was] the culmination of a decade of increasingly severe discriminatory, anti-Jewish measures implemented by the Nazis."[9]
>
> —US Holocaust Memorial Museum

Over time the Nazis came to view this approach to dealing with the Jews as too costly and time-consuming. So in January 1942, at Hitler's orders, several Nazi government officials and SS officers met in the Berlin suburb of Wannsee to discuss implementing the so-called Final Solution. This was the Nazi euphemism, or code name, for the plan to kill all the Jews in Europe. In the words of the curators of the US Holocaust Memorial Museum, that strategy was "the culmination of a decade of increasingly severe discriminatory, anti-Jewish measures implemented by the Nazis. Today, the 'Final Solution' is used as a synonym for the genocide of Europe's Jews."[9]

The Nazis who met at Wannsee grasped that transporting hundreds of thousands, and eventually millions, of Jews and other people to the death camps would be an immense task. The only cost-effective way to do it, they decided, was to employ trains. For that reason, the death camps in Poland were purposely built along the region's chief railway lines.

Nightmarish Journeys

The gruesome experience of the death camps nearly always began with a nightmarish journey aboard one of these trains. These journeys, which lasted from one to five days, have been well documented by the recollections of survivors, former German guards, and townspeople who witnessed them. In most cases people to be transported were herded into empty boxcars that normally carried cattle and other livestock. Typically, the guards shoved so many people into the cars that there was barely enough room to breathe.

In addition, there was no food or water provided on these transports, nor was there any heat in the winter or air-conditioning

Hungarian Jews are pictured getting off a train at Auschwitz-Birkenau. Within hours, most new arrivals at Auschwitz were dead.

Eradicating Disabled People

The first gas chambers and large ovens the Nazis employed to kill large numbers of people were not built explicitly to murder Jews. Rather, Nazi leaders initially envisioned constructing such extermination facilities to get rid of people who were mentally or physically disabled. In Nazi ideology, such individuals were seen as inferior and not worthy enough to live. The plan intended to eradicate them, hatched in the mid-1930s, came to be called the T-4, or euthanasia, program. (*Euthanasia* is the technical term for so-called mercy killing.) It was supervised by a team of German doctors, who toured hospitals and mental institutions to determine who among the disabled should be eliminated. According to the US Holocaust Memorial Museum:

> Doomed patients were transferred to six institutions in Germany and Austria, where they were killed in specially constructed gas chambers. Infants and small children with disabilities were also killed by injection with a deadly dose of drugs or by starvation. The bodies of the victims were burned in large ovens called *crematoria*. Despite public protests in 1941, the Nazi leadership continued this program in secret throughout the war. About 200,000 people with disabilities were murdered between 1940 and 1945.

US Holocaust Memorial Museum, "The Murder of People with Disabilities." https://encyclopedia.ushmm.org.

in the summer. Sanitation was nonexistent. The stench of excrement, urine, and sweat filled the air inside the rail cars. Twenty-seven-year-old Polish Jew Abram Krzepicki later described the terrible conditions he experienced on a railway car bound for Treblinka, saying, "The stink in the car was unbearable. People were defecating in all four corners of the car. . . . The men removed their shirts and lay half naked. Some of the women, too, took off their dresses and lay in their undergarments. People lay on the floor, gasping and shuddering as if feverish, laboring to get some air into their lungs."[10]

In these unbearable conditions, some of the passengers, especially elderly and infirm folk, became ill. Guards

"People lay on the floor, gasping and shuddering as if feverish, laboring to get some air into their lungs."[10]

—Polish Jew Abram Kszepicki describing the train ride to Treblinka periodically inspected the cars. Anyone who appeared to be too sick to make it to the destination was instantly killed.

Arrival at the Camps

As terrible as the journey aboard what came to be known as the death trains was, it did not come close to what lay ahead. Wieslaw Kielar, a Polish author and filmmaker who died in 1990, described what happened when he arrived at Auschwitz at age twenty-one. "Suddenly the doors of our carriage are flung open. Someone on the platform shouts at the top of his voice 'Everybody out! Get a move on, you shits.'" As people attempted to climb down out of the train, the guards would "bring the butts of their carbines down on our backs with resounding blows."[11]

At the time, the new arrivals had no way of knowing that within a couple of hours many of them would be dead. And of those who would be initially spared, most would be killed a few months or years later. The unfortunates pouring out of the train cars had no inkling that the Nazi regime and its many enablers would be among the most prolific mass murderers in human history.

CHAPTER TWO

The Barest Existence

Jadwiga Apostol, a teacher from Poland, was lucky. She survived three years in the Auschwitz death camp. One of her strongest memories from the terrible years 1942 to 1945, she said years later, was the haunting phantom of hunger—"hunger that was so merciless and so boundless, so inescapable; hunger that terrified you day and night with visions of death . . . [that] turned bread into something sacred."[12]

Scarce and Unpalatable Food

Memories of relentless, soul-crushing hunger have stayed with other survivors of the Nazi death camps. Many have described the yearning for food as worse than being confined or beaten. Melania Smierciak, another Auschwitz survivor, said that slow, steady starvation was a "concentration camp torment so enormous that people who have never gone through real hunger will [not] understand it."[13]

An unnamed Jewish survivor of the Treblinka death camp later recalled the typical meager rations that the inmates received. The food, she stated,

> was distributed only once a day, in the evening. Every man received six cooked potatoes with the peels still on them. In addition, [the camp guards] distributed a slice of bread, which was for the morning, and which we were not allowed to eat until then. As we

twisted and turned on the bunks at night, our insides were so empty that we couldn't stop thinking about that slice of bread until we broke off a piece . . . [which] tasted like clay and smelled like a sick animal.[14]

The quality and quantity of food given to death camp prisoners served a purpose. Many starved to death, but it kept some of them alive long enough to perform the menial tasks necessary to keep the camp running. Lack of food also ensured that the prisoners remained physically weak and therefore easier to manage and brutalize. As the scholars at the Holocaust Research Project explain:

> "As we twisted and turned on the bunks at night, our insides were so empty that we couldn't stop thinking about [a] slice of bread."[14]
>
> —A Jewish prisoner at Treblinka

The prisoners' daily diet contained less than a 1000 calories, well below the norm for people undertaking hard labour. . . . [Many] prisoners were [therefore] doomed to die, within a short space of time. On these rations after a short time the skin became grey-blue, grew thinner, became parchment-like, hardened then peeled off. . . . In the last phase of starvation, prisoners no longer felt hungry, [and] refused to accept any food. . . . Self-preservation vanished—they were past any help.[15]

Substandard Living Conditions

Partly because of this persistent lack of nutritious food, within a few weeks or months of the inmates' arrival, most had been reduced to sick and ghastly caricatures of their former selves. As scholars Eve N. Soumerai and Carol D. Schulz describe it, the average camp inmate was eventually "either bald or had a 'moldy' head and sickly yellow or gray skin. They had cuts and bruises from constant beatings, and sores and itching from insect bites, wooden shoes, and injuries at work. Their clothing was filthy, even when they tried to wash it, and they were covered with mud, grease, and blood. Diarrhea was a constant affliction, and everyone smelled awful."[16]

The prisoners knew full well how awful they looked and smelled. Moreover, their Nazi keepers knew that they knew and were pleased about it. Indeed, it was a calculated move by the SS guards to make the inmates appear, as well as feel, less than human. The Nazis reasoned, correctly, that the worse the prisoners felt about themselves, the more hopeless—and helpless—they would become.

This 1945 picture shows liberated prisoners of Wöbbelin concentration camp being taken to a hospital for medical attention. Many inmates starved to death, and others received only enough food to stay alive.

The Workday at Auschwitz

The workday for Auschwitz prisoners was often long and always tightly controlled. This summary of inmates' daily work routines comes from Germany's Auschwitz-Birkenau State Museum.

> The working day began at 4:30 in the summer and 5:30 in the winter. The prisoners got up at the sound of a gong and carefully tidied their living quarters. . . . At the sound of a second gong, they ran outside to the roll-call square, where they lined up in rows of ten by block. The prisoners were counted during roll call. If the numbers did not add up, roll call was prolonged. This could be especially tormenting for the prisoners, particularly in bad weather. Finally, the order came to form up by labor details. The prisoners walked out to working groups, with musical accompaniment in the form of marches played by the camp orchestra. . . .
>
> Prisoners performed various kinds of labor inside and outside the camp boundaries. From the end of March 1942, the minimum working day numbered 11 hours. Prisoners returned to the camp under SS escort before nightfall. They frequently carried the corpses of those who had died or been killed while laboring.

Auschwitz-Birkenau Memorial and Museum, "The Order of the Day," 2024. www.auschwitz.org.

Filth—along with bedbugs, fleas, mice, and rats—covered every inch of living space set aside for prisoners. Conditions worsened as time went on. Where once the dead had been buried or burned to ashes, prison guards were increasingly leaving human corpses outside or even inside the barracks to rot. A British medical officer, Hugh Glyn-Hughes, who helped liberate the Bergen-Belsen concentration camp in northern Germany in 1945, later recalled that he saw "piles of corpses lying all over the camp, some outside the [barbed] wire and some in between the huts . . . and the frightful scenes inside were much worse. . . . The gutters were full [of human remains] and within huts there were uncountable numbers of bodies, some even in the same bunks as the living. . . . [I also saw] an open pit half full of corpses."[17]

A truckload of bodies is shown in the Buchenwald camp in 1945 Germany. Guards often left human corpses outside or even in the barracks.

Barracks, Sleeping Areas, and Clothing

Even when free of decomposing corpses, the barracks reeked of filth and decay. Most of the barracks at Treblinka, Auschwitz, and other death camps were unadorned rectangular wooden buildings. When first erected, many of these structures had no bunks. As a result, the prisoners had to sleep on the wooden or earthen floors or in some cases on makeshift straw-filled mattresses. By midway through 1943, however, the barracks in most of the death camps had wooden bunks stacked in tiers, usually three or more high. A Jewish survivor of Auschwitz, Pincus Kolender, later remembered, "I would say there was about 300 or 400 men to a barrack. We had double, triple bunks. . . . [They] were actually single bunks, and two people had to sleep on it. It was bitter cold in the barracks, and we had to get up [at] 5:00 in the morning."[18]

"It was bitter cold in the barracks, and we had to get up [at] 5:00 in the morning."[18]

—Jewish Auschwitz inmate Pincus Kolender

Kolender's situation was actually better than that of most inmates. According to eyewitness testimony, often as many as four, five, or more prisoners were crammed into a single bunk measuring only a few feet wide. While helping liberate Bergen-Belsen, Glyn-Hughes was shocked and sickened when he saw the camp's barracks. The bunks, he said, "were filled absolutely to overflowing with prisoners in every state of emaciation and disease. There was not room for them to lie down at full length in each [bunk]. In the most crowded [buildings] there were anything from 600 to 1000 people in accommodation which should only have taken 100."[19]

Adding to the agony of the inmates' sleeping conditions was a lack of even the most basic comforts within the barracks. These structures had no heat, for example, even though subzero temperatures were common in the winter. The only means of warmth for the prisoners were their clothes and an occasional blanket, which invariably had to be shared with two or three other bedmates. Those blankets were never washed and became coated with spittle, blood, and human waste.

The clothing issued to inmates was equally shabby. It often bore signs of a former wearer's illness or death. Many death camp prisoners were given the blood-stained uniforms of dead Soviet soldiers to wear. Some received the remnants of clothing left behind by former inmates. Any clothes or shoes they received were typically ill-fitting and uncomfortable. Footwear ranged from simple wooden clogs to cheap leather shoes originally belonging to inmates who had died months or years before. Yet the common wisdom was that any sort of shoe was better than none at all because walking barefoot on the rocks and debris that littered the camps often caused injuries. The worst of those wounds sometimes became infected and led to death. Even in the death camps, where all were slated to die, a sliver of hope for life remained. For this reason, people feared infection.

Sanitation and Sickness

The camp inmates also feared the lack of proper sanitation. Many deaths resulted from the unsanitary conditions in the camps. At Majdanek, for example, there was a single washroom in a section of the facility containing at least forty-five hundred inmates. The term *washroom* is a misnomer, however, for the room had only two or three faucets, and the water they produced was not clean. Nor were there any soap, washcloths, or towels.

Even worse, most death camps had no toilets. Instead, they featured crude latrines consisting of long, deep ditches into which the prisoners relieved themselves. The guards permitted them to use those pits only twice during daylight hours and never at night. Thus, someone who needed to go after bedtime had to do so in a bucket that sat beside the bunks. If that receptacle was full, which it frequently was, he or she had no recourse but to use the floor. Glyn-Hughes described the appalling situation, saying that each Nazi camp was "absolutely one mass of human excreta. In the [barracks] themselves the floors were covered [with it], and the

This photo from the Auschwitz-Birkenau Museum in Poland shows a concentration camp latrine.

people in the top bunks who could not get out [of bed] just poured it onto the bunks below."[20]

Lack of sanitation frequently led to rampant spread of disease. Among the most common were typhoid fever and typhus, both caused by bacteria that thrive in contaminated water and human waste. Both lead to fever spikes that can kill if untreated, but treatment was not a priority in the death camps.

These were not the only illnesses that added to the misery of death camp inmates. Most prisoners developed dysentery (severe diarrhea) at one time or another. Also rampant were scabies, a serious skin infection caused by tiny parasites burrowing under the skin; tuberculosis, a frequently fatal lung disease; and gangrenous stomatitis, often called noma for short, an erosion of the facial tissues associated with malnutrition and poor sanitation.

Surrounded by all this sickness and suffering, the camp physicians typically refused to administer treatment to inmates who needed it. On the one hand, those doctors were there mainly to treat SS officers and German camp staff. On the other, Nazi camp physicians had no problem with allowing Jews and other prisoners to die. In fact, at times the camp doctors actually encouraged the spread of disease among the prisoners, seeing it as part of the strategy underpinning the very existence of the camps in the first place. Indeed, Soumerai and Schulz point out, one reason the extermination camps had been constructed "was to cause as many Jews as possible to die of what some have called 'natural extermination.' Its means included starvation, severe illness, and working inmates to the point of exhaustion and physical damage. Some high-ranking Nazis talked about transforming the prisoners into 'starving beasts' who would sooner or later simply drop dead."[21]

Teenaged Prisoners

The concept of natural extermination that had been part of the basic purpose of the camps all along was nowhere more starkly apparent than at the biggest and most famous of the Nazi camps—Auschwitz. There, as at nearly all the camps, it was expected that a given group of arriving prisoners would soon die off, to be replaced by a second group. And over time that new group would largely expire, to be replaced by a third group, and so forth.

The Nazis put that idea into practice even as the camp was being built. The very first prisoners shipped to Auschwitz were assigned the task of erecting the barracks and other structures that would house later prisoners. This was difficult, grueling work. Nazi leaders assigned it to large numbers of Jewish teenagers, who, it was assumed, would have the necessary strength and stamina. A further assumption was that those young people who died in the process could easily be replaced by later trainloads of Jews.

That first group of teens—consisting of 997 young Jewish women—arrived by train on March 27, 1942. They had been forcibly taken from their homes in villages in Slovakia, the small nation located directly south of Poland. (No one knows for sure why they were all girls. Some experts think the Nazis figured that girls would be less likely to violently resist while being kidnapped than boys.) As journalist Gillian Brockell summarizes it, their job was

> to build the very infrastructure that would convert the camp into a death machine. Over the next year, they were brutally forced to demolish old buildings with their bare hands, empty trash out of frozen lakes and build dozens of new barracks. For clothing, they were given the bloody uniforms of dead Soviet soldiers and a few striped dresses with no undergarments. Their entire bodies were shaved, and their shoes were flat pieces of wood with flimsy cloth ties.[22]

As expected, most of these young women died during their first year at Auschwitz. The few girls who did survive that ordeal

Driven to Eat Almost Anything

Starvation among prisoners was common in the death camps. The desperate need to survive drove some prisoners to eat anything they could find, including grass, tar, and earthworms. Polish Auschwitz survivor Stanisław Biedroń had the job of loading potatoes onto trucks for transport to the railway station. This job gave him a chance to eat rotting potatoes. Because the potatoes attracted mice, some inmates also caught and ate live mice. Prisoners who were found eating anything other than their usual rations, even rotten food and rodents, were severely punished, as Biedroń later explained.

> While on the job, we used to eat half-rotten potatoes; they tasted like salted gherkins [pickles]. Others ate raw mice—there were a lot of mice there. But if an SS-man caught a [prisoner] with a mouse or a rotten spud, he would beat him up and made him stand for twelve hours at the gate to the camp with that mouse or rotten potato. However, few if any could do it, and usually [an SS officer] would finish him off [by shooting him].

Quoted in Zdzislaw Jan Ryn and Stanisław Kłodziński, "Hunger in the Concentration Camps, Part 1," *Medical Review Auschwitz*, November 8, 2022. www.mp.pl.

were given other tasks. One particularly detestable one was to transfer bodies of Jews killed in the gas chambers to the crematoria. Incredibly, a handful of the girls managed to survive. Of the original 997, about 20 were still alive at the war's end. One, Edith Friedman Grosman, survived well into the twenty-first century. "I'm sure I've survived for a reason," she told an interviewer in 2017. "One of us had to still be here to tell you what happened."[23]

CHAPTER THREE

Processing Death

When Benjamin Lesser, a fifteen-year-old Polish Jew, exited the train that had brought him to the Auschwitz death camp, he was momentarily confused and disoriented. What was this place? he wondered. For a few minutes all that he could think about was the train trip he and his fellow Jews had just taken. "The conditions during what turned out to be a three-day journey," he said in a postwar interview, "were so inhumane, that I cannot find enough adjectives in all of the languages I speak to describe them."[24]

For a few more minutes, the young man stood in the midst of a large crush of people—all detainees like himself. They were packed together on a wide wooden platform that stretched out along the side of the motionless train. Suddenly, Lesser caught sight of a tall man who wore the universal symbol of medicine—two snakes winding around a winged staff—on his collar. Although the man's clothing also bore the SS insignia, Lesser thought that a man of medicine might see the benefits of keeping a young, healthy man like himself alive. Pushing his way through the crowd, Lesser approached the doctor and blurted out, "I am eighteen years old!" This was a lie. But the boy hoped he could pass for a somewhat older youth. "I am healthy," Lesser added. "And I can work!"[25]

The man, it turned out, was Josef Mengele, a notorious Nazi doctor who performed unspeakable medical experiments on hundreds of prisoners. Many were children, and almost all died at his hands. On this day, however, Mengele produced a toothy smile and gestured to Lesser to move to a line of people on the left.

The process by which Mengele directed Lesser toward the left, while other new arrivals moved into a second line on the right, was called "selection." In most cases those directed into the right-hand line—small children, elderly folk, and sick people—were deemed too weak to do hard labor. They were sent straight to their deaths. The rest—those in the left-hand line—were divided into groups. Some were separated by gender and others by physical strength; still others might be singled out for medical experiments by Mengele and other Nazi doctors. In whatever way they were separated, one thing everyone in the left line had in common was that they were slated to die, just like those in the right line. The difference was that the Nazis intended those on the left to die slowly, over the course of weeks, months, or longer, from starvation and overwork.

The separation process was agonizing, as people were frequently separated from their loved ones. Barbara Stimler, a Polish Jew who arrived at age sixteen at Auschwitz in 1943, later told how the Nazi guards

> "The husbands were [torn] from wives, the mothers from sons, it was just a nightmare."[26]
>
> —Polish Jew Barbara Stimler on arriving at Auschwitz in 1943

started separating women from men. Cries. It was just terrible. The husbands were [torn] from wives, the mothers from sons, it was just a nightmare. I started to get diarrhoea. . . . We started going through the gate; the SS men were on both sides. . . . I went to the right, they told me to go to the right. . . . I cannot explain to you the cries and the screams, and [people] tearing their hair off. Can you imagine?[26]

Chosen to Work

Once the new arrivals had been separated into groups, those chosen for induction into a camp were herded into processing areas. The SS men had chosen them to do daily work to support the Nazi regime and its war effort. Most often such slave labor consisted of digging ditches, removing large rocks from quarries, and doing heavy lifting in German armaments factories that had been built beside or very near the camps.

Before that work began, however, the new arrivals had to go through a lengthy induction process. They were forced to give up all their personal belongings, including money, jewelry, coats, shoes, eyeglasses, and family keepsakes. Anyone who refused to comply or tried to hide objects from the guards was soundly beaten. It was useless to hide things anyway, since all new inmates had to remove all their clothing during the first few hours after they arrived, and the guards ruthlessly and thoroughly searched all body cavities to find anything that might be concealed.

During the phase of the induction process in which the new arrivals were stripped naked, they had to take cold showers. The water was sometimes laced with disinfectants. One survivor of Auschwitz, Lilly Malnik, later recalled the shame and embarrass-

This 1944 photo shows the "selection" process of Hungarian Jews who have arrived at Auschwitz-Birkenau.

ment she felt over this episode of forced nakedness. "They made us feel like [we] were animals," she said. The Nazi guards "were walking around and laughing and looking at us, and you take a young girl at that age who has never been exposed to a person, to a man, and you stay there naked. I wanted [that] the ground should open and I should go in it."[27]

After these showers—the only ones they would ever have in the camp—the new inmates had their heads, and in some cases their entire bodies, shaved. In 1944 a Jew from Prague, Czechoslovakia, Hana Bruml, then twenty-two, endured this indignity during her first day at Auschwitz. "We went to a room where they shaved us," she recalled after the war. "They also shaved our pubic hair—about a hundred people with one blade, [and there was] no cleanliness otherwise."[28]

At this point, the new inmates were given dirty, ill-fitting clothes to wear and assigned to various barracks and work gangs. Many of these individuals would die from starvation, malnutrition, disease, hard labor, torture, or brutality. But in some sense they were the lucky ones.

Death by Gassing

In contrast to the camp workers who had originally been directed into the left-hand line upon arrival, prisoners who had been sent into the right-hand line had zero chance of survival. Leaving the railway platform, they were herded along wooden walkways until they saw a large building up ahead made of concrete and brown stones. The SS men guiding them explained that they would now be given showers to make sure they were clean when they settled into the camp.

The prisoners entered the building a few hundred at a time. Members of such a group were ordered to remove all their clothes and hand over any and all personal items. Sometimes they each received a small bar of soap. Then the SS men steered them into a very large shower facility with many showerheads projecting from the side walls.

Confiscated Belongings

When Jews and other people destined to die arrived at the death camps, they were forced to hand over all belongings they had brought with them. Those objects were piled up and then shipped to a warehouse or other storage facility. Agents of the German government later sold most of the items and deposited the profits into one of the Nazis' treasuries. Some idea of the tremendous volume of such plunder can be seen in the number of objects collected in the Majdanek camp in a single day—July 20, 1943. According to the detailed records of the camp's SS guards, the haul on that day included 2,150 men's coats and jackets; 3,900 women's jackets; and tens of thousands of shoes, women's dresses and scarves, and watches and other pieces of jewelry. "Even the prisoners' hair, cut upon their admission to the camp, was of value to the Third Reich," the Holocaust Research Project points out. The hair was used to make "socks for [German] submarine crews."

Holocaust Research Project, "Majdanek Concentration Camp (a.k.a. Lublin KL): Reception, Prisoners Daily Life, Sub-camps," 2007. www.holocaustresearchproject.org.

What the recent arrivals did not know was that they had been tricked. The huge room in which they stood only looked like a large-scale shower. In reality, it was one of the chief means of mass murder employed by the Nazis—a lethal gas chamber.

Josef Paczynski, a Polish inmate at Auschwitz, witnessed the gassing of new arrivals at the camp. "I went into the attic of that building," he later remembered, and "I could see everything that was going on." After all the victims had been packed into the chamber, Paczynski went on, "an SS man climbed onto the flat roof . . . put on a gas mask, opened the hatch and dropped the powder in. When he did this . . . you could hear a great scream from within. . . . In order to stifle the screaming they had two motorcycles standing on the pavement [nearby, with the] engines revved up as far as they could go, to stifle the screams."[29]

After the war Auschwitz's commandant, Rudolf Höss, gave a description of such gassings. His account matched Paczynski's very closely. The screaming went on for fifteen minutes or so, Höss recalled. "We knew when the people were dead because their screaming stopped. . . . [Then] we opened the doors and removed the bodies."[30] Höss also provided details about the powder Paczynski saw an SS officer pour into a hatch located above the gas chamber. It was hydrogen cyanide, which the Nazis called Zyklon B. Taking the form of bluish-colored crystals, it emitted fumes that caused a person to die rapidly after inhaling it.

These gassings of prisoners were the hideous end product of a series of experiments the Nazis had earlier done with extermination methods. These techniques were not initially intended to kill large numbers of Jews, prisoners of war, and other supposed enemies of the German people. Rather, the earliest Nazi uses of poison gas to kill people developed as part of a secret program called T-4. The object was to find efficient ways to eliminate members of German society whom Hitler and his chief henchmen deemed unworthy of life—principally physically handicapped and mentally ill people. Later, the regime expanded on the idea and

> "We knew when the people [inside the gas chambers] were dead because their screaming stopped."[30]
>
> —Longtime Auschwitz commandant Rudolf Höss

Lethal gas chambers were one of the Nazis' chief means of mass murder. The entrance to the Auschwitz gas chamber is shown here.

employed gas to kill millions of so-called enemies and inferiors. The obscene goal evolved into making the mass murder as large-scale and efficient as possible.

Bullets vs. Gas

Poison gas was by no means the only method the Nazis used to commit mass murders. During the war's early stages, for example, they eradicated large numbers of prisoners by shooting them. Death squads called *Einsatzgruppen* lined up the victims beside or inside ditches, opened fire on them with various kinds of guns, and buried the bodies in those ditches. Later in the war, the Nazis left piles of corpses outside to rot. But throughout most

During the early stages of the war, Nazi death squads lined up victims beside ditches, shot them, then buried the bodies. This photo shows Babi Yar, a ravine in the Ukrainian city of Kyiv, where a number of massacres were carried out.

of the conflict, they buried the evidence of their actions to prevent exposing Hitler's lies that no such atrocities were occurring.

Of the several surviving eyewitness accounts of these large-scale killings, one of the more detailed came from Erwin Bingel, a German army officer. He saw some twenty-four thousand Jews slaughtered in the Russian town of Uman on September 16, 1941. "One row of Jews was ordered to move forward," he wrote in a statement after the war,

> "Mothers [were not] spared the terrible sight of their children being gripped by their little legs and put to death with one stroke of the pistol-butt or club."[31]
>
> —German army officer Erwin Bingel on the Nazis' mass shootings of Jews

and [they] had to undress completely and hand over everything they wore and carried. . . . Then [they] were made to stand in line in front of the ditches, irrespective of their sex. The commandos then marched in behind the line and began [shooting]. . . . Even women carrying children . . . were not spared this horrible ordeal. Nor were mothers spared the terrible sight of their children being gripped by their little legs and put to death with one stroke of the pistol-butt or club, thereafter to be thrown on the heap of human bodies in the ditch. . . . The people in the first row thus having been killed in the most inhuman manner, those of the second row were now ordered to step forward. . . . The air resounded with the cries of children and the tortured.[31]

Although such mass shootings continued to occur as the war dragged on, leading Nazis felt that they were not effective enough. The many thousands of bullets required were expensive and could be put to better use on the battlefield, they said. Plus, Himmler and other top Nazis saw that killing unarmed civilians at close range traumatized many of the conscripted German soldiers involved.

Initially, the solution seemed to be mobile trucks in which victims could be gassed to death using the carbon monoxide emitted in the vehicles' exhaust. Gasoline was cheaper than bullets.

A Cruel Ruse

When trains filled with Jews and other prisoners arrived at the death camps, a hefty proportion of them were gassed to death within two or three hours. The Nazis who ran the camps wanted this monstrous process to proceed efficiently and without resistance, which meant that the prisoners needed to be kept in the dark about their fate. Therefore, the SS officers routinely used a cruel ruse designed to keep these condemned individuals from realizing they were about to enter an extermination unit. During his trial for war crimes, Rudolf Höss, the longest-serving commander of Auschwitz, later described this ruse. "At Auschwitz, we endeavored to fool the victims into thinking that they were to go through a delousing process." Part of the diversion in Höss's facility consisted of signs posted on the railway platforms. These signs read:

> You are in a transit camp, from which you will be sent to a labor camp. In order to avoid epidemics, you must present your clothing and belongings for immediate disinfection. Gold, money, foreign currency, and jewelry should be deposited with the cashiers in return for a receipt. They will be returned to you later when you present the receipt. Bodily cleanliness requires that everyone bathe before continuing the journey.

Quoted in William L. Shirer, *The Rise and Fall of the Third Reich: A History of Nazi Germany*. Greenwich, CT: Fawcett, 1960, p. 969.

Quoted in Yitzhak Arad, *Belzec, Sobibor, Treblinka: The Operation Reinhard Death Camps*. Bloomington: University of Indiana Press, 1987, pp. 83–84.

Also, no ordinary soldiers were needed. The work could be done by battle-hardened SS officers, most of whom had no qualms about murdering defenseless people.

A Massive Murder Apparatus

In practice, the trucks proved to be an effective method of killing people. The Nazis identified one major drawback, however. Each vehicle held only a small number of people. Once the decision to eradicate people by the millions had been made, a more efficient method was needed. The solution was to continue employing gas but on a much larger scale. Bigger gas chambers were erected in some of the concentration camps. The most massive gassing facilities were in Auschwitz and the other five extermination camps. In addition, about ten of the numerous other concentration camps had smaller gas chambers.

This steady progression of experimentation with killing methods shows that mass murder became increasingly like a science to the Nazi regime. The same can be said of the problem of disposing of the corpses after the gassings. Here, the answer became multiple crematoria, or large ovens. For the most part, the SS men did not themselves collect the corpses from the gas chambers, put them in the ovens, and burn them. Instead, they forced small squads of inmates, mostly Jews, to carry out that disgusting task. These inmates were called *Sonderkommandos*, or "special commandos." The SS officers periodically killed these commandos, whose bodies were then burned by newly trained squads of inmates. In this way the SS guards kept their hands clean while making sure to fulfill the primary purpose of the death camps.

Resistance and Rebellion

Rudolf Vrba, age nineteen, and Alfred Wetzler, then age twenty-five, could see the moon shining brightly in a clear sky on the evening of April 10, 1944. The two Slavic Jews lay on their backs, staring upward from the bottom of a shallow hole dug in a field several hundred yards outside the walls of the Auschwitz death camp. A few hours before, they had done something that both the camp's overseers and its inmates had thought impossible. The two young men had managed to elude the SS men guarding the camp's perimeter, slip through the outer fence, and escape into the open meadows surrounding the facility.

Vrba and Wetzler had planned their escape carefully. They had based their strategy mostly on information from inmates who had been in the camp for a long time and had observed how the Nazis reacted to escape attempts. In this way Vrba and his companion learned that timing was essential in all stages of the escape. First, they chose a time of day when the SS men would be preoccupied with various daily duties and not notice their absence immediately. That would give the would-be escapees a few hours' head start. The two men had also been advised that the Nazis who would try to hunt them down would expect the escapees to get as far away from the camp as quickly as possible. So the pursuers would initially concentrate their search on the countryside several miles from Auschwitz. Furthermore, if the

In 1964 Rudolf Vrba (shown) appeared before the grand jury in Frankfurt, Germany, to testify against the accused former SS guards of the Auschwitz extermination camp. Having escaped from Auschwitz in 1944, he was among the first-known escapees.

escapees could not be found after three days, Vrba and Wetzler were told, the Nazi authorities would no longer search in the region where the camp lay.

Hence, Vrba and Wetzler purposely remained in the hole in the meadow just outside the camp for three agonizing days and nights. They had no food or water. And they remained almost totally motionless. After three days, their muscles had begun to atrophy. Somehow, they were able to muster the strength to endure this ordeal and eventually emerged from their hiding place. Through stealth and much good luck, after several weeks they made it to Slovakia (located just north of Hungary), a region the Soviets were then in the process of liberating. In this way, Vrba and Wetzler became the first-known Auschwitz inmates to make it out of the camp and to survive beyond the war's end.

It is a testament to the two men's courage and desire to help other Jews survive that they did not seek to remain in safety. Instead, in late 1944 they joined a resistance group with which they tirelessly fought the Nazis until Germany's defeat in April 1945.

Other Daring Escapes

There were also a number of escapes from other Nazi death camps. On September 13, 1942, for example, Polish Jew Abram

Krzepicki managed to make it out of the Treblinka death camp. Along with other prisoners, he had been ordered to load a railway car with the clothes of inmates murdered in the gas chambers. When the guards overseeing these inmates looked away for a moment, Krzepicki jumped into one of the other cars and hid. Once the train was at a safe distance from Treblinka, he jumped out and made his way to safety. Soon afterward, he joined the Polish underground (native Poles who secretly resisted the Nazi tyranny).

Similarly, Polish Jew Szlamek Bajler, a prisoner at the Chelmno death camp in central Poland, escaped on January 19, 1942. He and a few other inmates had been placed in a bus that carried them to a field outside the camp. They were ordered to dig a pit in which to throw the bodies of inmates who had been executed for trying to escape. After the job was finished, on the way back to camp Bajler jumped from a small window in the side of the bus. "When I hit the ground," he later recalled, "I rolled for a bit and scraped the skin off my hands. The only thing that mattered to me was not to break a leg. I turned round to see if they had noticed . . . but [the bus] continued its journey. I lost no time but ran as fast as I could across fields and woods."[32]

> "When I hit the ground, I rolled for a bit and scraped the skin off my hands."[32]
>
> —Polish Jew Szlamek Bajler describing his escape from Chelmno

Risking All at Treblinka

Escapes were not the only form of resistance in the death camps. Some prisoners fought back courageously within the camps by refusing to follow the guards' orders or by purposely breaking camp rules. These brave individuals were invariably beaten, tortured, and executed.

The boldest and fiercest resistance by inmates took the form of large-scale rebellions in three of the death camps. The first took place at Treblinka. In early 1943 a secret resistance group had formed at Treblinka. At first it consisted of only a handful of inmates, but over time hundreds of others joined the plot. The first

The Dressmakers of Auschwitz

In addition to escape attempts and open rebellion, the prisoners in the Nazi death camps employed other forms of resistance. One of the most subtle yet effective was engineered by Jewish inmate Marta Fuchs. Shortly after she arrived at Auschwitz in 1943, the camp commandant's wife, Hedwig Höss, discovered that Fuchs was a skilled seamstress. Fuchs was then pressed into service making dresses for Höss and the wives of other camp officers. That dressmaking operation came to be called the Upper Tailoring Studio.

While running the so-called studio Fuchs saw an opportunity to resist the camp's brutal system by helping other female inmates survive. She did this by convincing Höss to let her recruit more seamstresses from among the prisoners. By mid-1944, twenty-five women were working with Fuchs as seamstresses. Thanks to their new status in the camp, they were allowed to shower regularly and received adequate food rations. Most importantly, all of them survived Auschwitz and the war, thanks to the efforts of Marta Fuchs.

issue to address was how to eliminate as many of the SS guards as possible. According to historian Yitzhak Arad, a noted expert on the Nazi camps, the decision was made to attack the guards

> during the day, when they were scattered throughout the camp, [and] not grouped together. With the proper planning and organization, they could all be overcome at the same time. . . . The final plan called for taking control of the camp, setting it on fire, and only then abandoning it. The planners believed that their numerical superiority . . . and the element of surprise would give them a good chance of succeeding.[33]

The uprising erupted on August 2, 1943. Per the plan, some inmates assaulted SS men, although a fair number of those Nazis survived. The rebels did succeed in torching many of the camp's buildings. Then a large mass of

> "The planners believed that . . . the element of surprise would give them a good chance of succeeding."[33]
>
> —Historian Yitzhak Arad on the Treblinka uprising

them rushed the main gate. Many were cut down by machine guns, but a few hundred made it through the gate and fanned out into the countryside. Of those escapees, roughly half were hunted down by Nazi authorities and slain. Meanwhile, when SS reinforcements arrived and secured the facility, they slaughtered all of the prisoners who had not been killed in the revolt. Yet the camp was so badly damaged that Himmler and other top Nazis decided to close it down. Thus, those inmates who gave their lives in that effort did strike a resounding blow to the Nazi regime and its program of genocide.

Insurgency at Sobibor

A few months after the Treblinka insurrection, a similar and more successful rebellion took place at Sobibor, situated about 3 miles (4.8 km) west of the Bug River, which formed Poland's eastern border. The gas chambers and crematoria at Sobibor began operation in May 1942. Before the uprising occurred, some two hundred thousand people had been murdered there.

Appalled at what was happening in the facility, sometime in the early fall of 1943, several concerned inmates formed a secret resistance group. Its leaders were Leon Feldhendler, a Polish Jew, and Alexander "Sasha" Pechersky, a Soviet Jewish military officer. One of the key events that motivated them was the camp's recent gassing of some twenty-seven hundred Russian Jews, many of them former Soviet soldiers. Pechersky argued that besides himself, there were a number of other former military men still alive in Sobibor. They would be a match for the SS guards in a fight, he told Feldhendler, so the sooner they launched an insurgency the better. Feldhendler agreed, and in historian Jason Dawsey's words, "the two men conceived one of the most daring plans of the Second World War."[34]

The goal they set for themselves was the liberation of all the camp's prisoners, then numbering six hundred, at one time. Part one of the plan was to stealthily gather whatever weapons they could. These included knives, axes, razors, and a few single-shot

Camp guards at Bergen-Belsen are pictured in 1945. Some prisoners fought back within the camps by refusing to follow the guards' orders or even fomenting rebellions.

rifles. Part two consisted of luring the most dangerous SS officers into the camp's workshops and quietly killing them there. Runners would then alert the rest of the inmates, and at a given signal everyone would assault the main gate.

The uprising began in the late afternoon of October 14, 1943. As planned, some inmates convinced several SS officers to enter workshops where secretly armed prisoners awaited. Of special import was luring Johann Niemann, the SS deputy commandant, into the tailors' shop. Yehuda Lerner, a Jew who had been forced to make clothes for SS men, later recalled, "We had prepared axes, which we had sharpened. . . . The first [SS man] to arrive was Niemann. . . . I was sitting and sewing a button [on a coat and] the ax was between my legs. I got up, keeping the coat over the ax, approached the SS man from behind, and split his head."[35]

> "I got up, keeping the coat over the ax, approached the SS man from behind, and split his head."[35]
>
> —Yehuda Lerner, an inmate who took part in the Sobibor revolt

Paving the Way to Freedom

After the war, Alexander "Sasha" Pechersky, one of the leaders of the uprising at Sobibor, gave an interview to a group of Holocaust researchers known as the Holocaust Education and Archive Research Team. In that interview he described the courage and heroism of various inmates who fought the better-armed Nazis to a near-standstill during the Sobibor revolt.

The guards on the watchtower opened intensive machine-gun fire on the escaping prisoners. The guards who were at and between the barbed-wire fences joined them. Yanek the [Jewish] carpenter aimed and shot at the guards on the watchtower, [and] the machine-gun fell silent. The locksmith Henrick used the captured sub-machine gun to silence the gunner from the second watchtower. . . . The remaining SS men tried with automatic fire to cut off the way of the crowd of prisoners. . . . The main body of the prisoners turned toward the fences. . . . Many [prisoners] found their death there, but they paved the way to freedom for the prisoners who followed them. . . . I was one of the last to leave the camp.

Quoted in Holocaust Education and Archive Research Team, "Alexander Pechersky on the Revolt and Escape from the Sobibor Death Camp," 2011. www.holocaustresearchproject.org.

After about a dozen leading SS officers had been eliminated, per the plan, runners informed the rest of the inmates, who now tensely awaited Pechersky's signal. He waited a few more minutes to hear that two prisoners had cut the telegraph and telephone cables to keep the remaining guards from calling for help. Then he gave the attack order, and from all directions inmates surged into the open area near the main gate. As they charged forward, Pechersky called out, "Death to the fascists!" Seconds later he added, "Let the world know what happened here!"[36]

Results of Resistance

The results of the Sobibor revolt were, like the one at Treblinka, mixed. An estimated three hundred inmates, approximately half of those incarcerated at Sobibor, managed to escape. Of those, a majority were later captured and killed in the huge Nazi manhunt that followed the outbreak. But fifty-eight more-fortunate individuals, including Pechersky, made it to freedom and survived the war.

As happened at Treblinka, the SS closed and dismantled the Sobibor camp after the rebellion. This action resulted in part because, at the time, the Soviet army was making gains to the east of Bug River. The Nazis did not want the enemy to see the evidence of the atrocities they had committed there. To that end, they forced the prisoners to bury bodies and other evidence of war crimes in unmarked locations.

Rumors of the advancing Soviets steadily filtered into the other death camps. Hoping that Soviet troops would soon liberate Auschwitz, in the summer of 1944 some of its prisoners formed a secret resistance group. Three Jewish women who were forced to manufacture munitions at the camp were able to smuggle and hide small caches of gunpowder. And when the prisoners launched a revolt on October 7, some of them managed to blow up one of the camp's crematoria. They also employed rocks and

This photo shows a monument to Alexander Pechersky, one of the leaders of the 1943 uprising at the Sobibor camp.

«Г... ...сила людей, кото... ...ми руками шли ... ...я руково... ...етского лейтенан... ...Печерского. Это не може... ...щать и удивлять».

В.В. Путин.

ПЕЧЕРСКИЙ

ПЕЧЕРСКИЙ
Александр Аронов...

hammers to attack several SS men and killed three of them. Although a few inmates made it outside the outer fences, they were quickly caught and executed, and the short-lived rebellion collapsed.

Although none of the three uprisings was completely successful, they did show that many of the death camp prisoners were willing to resist and, if necessary, die to save themselves and others. In the long run the closure of the Treblinka and Sobibor camps was significant. Without their means of mass death, the Nazis' application of their repugnant Final Solution slowed down.

In addition, if there had been any doubt in anyone's mind about the Nazi regime's barbaric nature, its reaction to the Sobibor revolt dispelled such notions. Following that incident, which embarrassed and angered the top Nazis, Himmler launched Operation Harvest Festival. The picturesque name masked its overt savagery. Jews and other inmates from multiple concentration camps were herded into the Majdanek camp. And there, on November 3, 1943, a small army of SS men took their revenge by strangling, clubbing, and shooting the half-starved, defenseless prisoners. In this event of "unspeakable horror," Dawsey writes, some 18,400 people perished. "No other massacre by the Nazis . . . in one location and in one twenty-four [hour] period matched it during the Holocaust. . . . With Harvest Festival, the Nazis established a new benchmark for radical evil."[37]

CHAPTER FIVE

Downfall of the Camps and Liberation

In April 1945, with Hitler's Third Reich in a state of collapse and chaos, American and other Allied forces swept into Germany and Poland, liberating concentration and death camps as they went. The sights that greeted the liberators were the same in all of the camps—grim, stomach-churning, heartrending testaments to the shocking inhumanity of the Nazi regime.

American soldier Leon Bass later recalled what he saw on entering the camp at Buchenwald, near the German city of Weimar. "When I walked through that gate," he said in a later interview,

> I saw in front of me what I call the walking dead. I saw human beings [who] had been beaten, had been starved. . . . They'd been denied everything, everything that would make anyone's life livable. They were standing in front of me and they were skin and bone. They had skeletal faces with deep-set eyes. . . . They were standing there, and they were holding on to one another just to keep from falling.[38]

As he continued to tour the camp along with the other Americans, Bass was struck by the sores on the bodies of virtually all the inmates. One of the medics in his unit told him these were clear signs of extreme malnutrition. Clearly, the prisoners had been starved nearly to death. Bass noticed that the scabs from the sores had caused one inmate's fingers to permanently stick together, robbing him of the use of his hand. "Oh, my God," Bass later exclaimed, "I'd seen nothing like this in all my life." It was simply "beyond anything in my experience."[39]

Bass's descriptions, given in interviews in the decades after the war, were corroborated by the thousands of other soldiers who liberated the Nazi camps and by the journalists who accompanied them. The leader of the American and European Allied forces and future US president, Dwight D. Eisenhower, himself toured one of Buchenwald's sub-camps. In a postwar interview, he said,

I have never felt able to describe my emotional reactions when I first came face to face with indisputable evidence of Nazi brutality and ruthless disregard of every shred of decency. . . . I have never at any other time experienced an equal sense of shock. I visited every nook and cranny of the camp because I felt it my duty to be [able] to testify at firsthand about these things in case there ever grew up at home the belief [that] the stories of Nazi brutality were just propaganda.[40]

Accompanying Eisenhower were other US generals, including George S. Patton. Widely known for his courage and toughness, Patton fought to keep himself from vomiting. Shocked to his core, he later called it "one of the most appalling sights that I have ever seen."[41]

Orders to Dismantle the Camps

Allied Soviet soldiers saw similar gruesome sights when they reached Poland, except at two of the death camps, Treblinka and Sobibor. By the time the Soviets reached the sites of these camps,

In 1945, American and other Allied forces liberated camps throughout Germany and Poland. This photo shows starved prisoners at Ebensee camp in Austria, at the time of liberation.

both were mostly gone, having been largely dismantled in the preceding few months. Hoping to prevent evidence of their mass murders from reaching the world, the Nazis began demolishing several of the death camps once defeat appeared imminent.

That demolition process was partially successful because nearly all of the murdered inmates had been buried or burned to ashes. As a result, for several decades the principal evidence of the mass murders that occurred at Treblinka was derived from two sources: the testimony of Jewish survivors and the admissions of some of the Nazi SS officers who had run the camp. In 2012, however, modern forensic experts discovered some previously hidden mass graves at the site that show conclusively that it was an extermination camp.

Nazi efforts to dismantle Auschwitz, the largest of the death camps, began in November 1944—about six months before Germany's declared defeat. The breakdown of the camp proceeded

Reams of Evidence

When Dwight D. Eisenhower compiled his eyewitness testimony of the Nazi camps, he correctly foresaw a sad future development. It was that some misguided individuals might claim that the Nazis' mass murders had never occurred. Often called "Holocaust denial," that idea ignores the fact that the Nazis' atrocities are among the most thoroughly documented events of modern history. In addition to the eyewitness reports of tens of thousands of surviving Jews, Poles, Gypsies, Russians, and many other victims, the reams of evidence include the physical remains of gas chambers and crematoria; thousands of photos and films taken by the Nazis themselves; and the testimony of many German soldiers, SS officers, and Nazi leaders who later admitted their roles in the slaughter. One of the most damning of such admissions was that of Auschwitz's commander, Rudolf Höss, who after the war said, "I was responsible for carrying out part of the cruel plans of the Third Reich for human destruction. . . . May the Lord God forgive one day what I have done. . . . May the facts which are now coming out about [those] horrible crimes . . . make the repetition of such cruel acts impossible for all time."

Quoted in John J. Hughes, "A Mass Murderer Repents: The Case of Rudolf Höss, Commandant of Auschwitz," Seton Hall University, March 25, 1998. www.shu.edu.

slowly, however, and it was not until January 1945 that a demolition crew blew up two of the camp's five crematoria. Hoping to erase as much evidence of war crimes as possible, groups of SS men burned camp documents in big bonfires. They also set fire to the enormous complex of structures in which they had stored the luggage and other property they had earlier plundered from the doomed inmates. While this was happening, Himmler ordered the destruction of all the remaining gas chambers and crematoria in the death camps.

One problem remained, however. Namely, what should be done with prisoners who had not yet been exterminated? The solution adopted by Himmler and other leading Nazis was to march the inmates westward and place them in some of the concentration camps in Germany. Himmler curtly warned the commanders of the death camps in Poland, "The Führer [Hitler] holds you personally responsible for . . . making sure that not a single prisoner from the [Polish camps] falls alive into the hands of the enemy."[42]

To ensure this directive would be followed, on January 17, 1945, SS officers began evacuating some of the more than one hundred thousand inmates still alive in Auschwitz. To start the process, approximately sixty thousand prisoners, most of them Jews, were herded out of the camp's gates and forced at gunpoint to march toward the west—the direction of Germany. This march, like others that originated from other Nazi camps, was a ruthless affair in which no thought was given to the prisoners' welfare or safety. Most had no coats to protect them from the severe winter cold, and many dropped dead of exposure. Also, the marchers received no food for days on end, causing some to perish from starvation. At the same time, anyone who could not keep up the pace set by the SS overseers was promptly shot in the head. An estimated fifteen thousand former Auschwitz inmates died in this march alone.

Nazis collected piles of luggage from prisoners upon their arrival at Auschwitz. Just before Germany's defeat, in an effort to erase evidence of war crimes, SS soldiers attempted to burn the structures in which they had stored the luggage.

All the Camps Liberated

In the weeks that followed, several of the extermination facilities in Poland were indeed destroyed, and many thousands of inmates were removed from the region and relocated. Yet the Nazis' attempts to cover up their war crimes ultimately failed. Their demolition teams did not have time to dismantle all the camps; for instance, large sections of Auschwitz remained intact. In addition, when the westward marches of camp inmates had begun in mid-January 1945, about nine thousand of those in Auschwitz had been deemed too sick to move. So they had been left there to die. Roughly two thousand of them did perish in the days that followed. But the other seven thousand were still alive when the Soviets liberated the camp on January 27.

The reason that the Nazis were unable to destroy all their camps was that the Allies invaded Germany and the lands bordering it far faster than Hitler and his generals had anticipated. One by one, Germany's land forces were crushed. And with the Nazi command structure falling apart, on April 30, 1945, Hitler committed suicide, leaving his defeated nation in ruins. As a result of Nazi Germany's swift and utter collapse, the Allies were able to liberate all the remaining concentration camps by May 1945.

> "Staggering out to meet [the Allied liberators] were the walking skeletons—human beings whose bodies were stripped of flesh."[43]
>
> —Historian Louis L. Snyder

Among the officers, soldiers, and supporting staffs of the liberating armies, each and every man and woman reacted similarly to the horrors they witnessed in those facilities. In the words of the late World War II historian Louis L. Snyder:

Battle-hardened veterans, inured to the sight and smell of death, were sickened. . . . They could scarcely believe their eyes. But there was the evidence—rows of incinerators, gas chambers disguised as shower rooms, thousands of bodies piled up like logs, others cast into pits and trenches. And staggering out to meet them were the walking skeletons—human beings whose bodies were stripped of flesh. . . . Strong men wept in the presence of this miserable army of unfortunates.[43]

The liberators were also aghast when they found out about the atrocities that had been performed by Josef Mengele and as many as two hundred other Nazi doctors in the camps. Using prisoners, including many children, as guinea pigs, they amputated hands, arms, and legs—without giving the victims anesthetics—and tried to sew those body parts onto other amputees. Other typical experiments included seeing how long people could live after having gasoline injected into them and killing Jews and Gypsies and dissecting their bodies in search of the "proof" that they were inferior to Aryans.

Germans Who Learned the Awful Truth

When the Nazi camps were liberated, the American generals who took part felt it was important for the German people to see for themselves the horrors their leaders had perpetrated. American troops rounded up some twelve hundred average German citizens from the towns surrounding the Buchenwald camp and took them on a tour of that facility. These Germans saw for themselves the torture rooms, dissection rooms, crematoria, and piles of corpses of people who had clearly been starved to death. As reported by American journalist Gene Currivan, who witnessed the visit:

The German people saw all this today, and they wept. Those who didn't weep were ashamed. . . . Some Germans were skeptical at first, as if this show had been staged for their benefit, but they were soon convinced. . . . Men turned white and women turned away. It was too much for them. These persons, who had been fed Nazi propaganda since 1933, were beginning to see the light. They were seeing with their own eyes what no quantity of American propaganda could convince them of. Here was what their own government had perpetrated.

Quoted in Louis L. Snyder, *The War: A Concise History, 1939–1945*. New York: Julian Messner, 1961, p. 425.

Personal Memories of Liberation

As for the prisoners whom the Allies liberated, their reactions were often a mix of contradictory feelings. On the one hand, they were clearly overjoyed at being rescued. On the other, expressions of that joy were tempered by the knowledge of so many others lost, the endurance of unspeakable acts, and bodies and minds too weak and too sick to celebrate survival. Renowned American journalist Edward R. Murrow was with the American troops who liberated Buchenwald in April 1945. His moving report reads in part:

> Men and boys reached out to touch me. They were in rags and the remnants of uniforms. Death already had marked many of them, but they were smiling with their eyes. . . . [I] asked to see one of the barracks [and] when I entered, men crowded around, tried to lift me to their shoulders. They were too weak. Many of them could not get out of bed. . . . As we walked out into the courtyard, a man fell dead. Two others, they must have been over 60, were crawling toward the latrine.[44]

Meanwhile, those former inmates who were physically able to do so greeted the liberators with cheers, hugs, and kisses. In addition, thousands of personal stories emerged from the scenes of liberation. One was that of Auschwitz survivor Paula Lebovics, who was only eleven at the time. For the rest of her life she never forgot how a Russian soldier with tears flowing down his cheeks smiled broadly at her and gave her a big hug. Then he offered her some food and she wondered to herself, "You mean somebody out there cares about me?"[45]

Another former prisoner, Polish Jew Gerda Weissmann, languished in several different labor camps before being rescued at age twenty-one by American soldiers. One of those men, Kurt Klein, treated her with the utmost respect and courtesy. "He held

the door open for me and let me precede him, and restored me to humanity again," she later recalled. "And he has been holding the door open for me for 50 years."[46] The two, she said, fell in love almost instantly, married less than a year later, and settled in the United States.

Also memorable is the story of Leon Bass and Robert Waisman. Bass, a Black American soldier who helped liberate the Buchenwald camp and described the inmates there as the "walking dead," left that place a changed man. "I was not the same anymore," he said many years later. "I realized now that human suffering is not relegated to just me. Oh, no. . . . We all become damaged by the evil of racism and anti-Semitism, bigotry, [and] prejudice."[47]

What Bass did not realize at the time was that as he toured Buchenwald, he was closely watched by Waisman, then a starving sixteen-year-old Jewish inmate. On April 11, 1945, at 3:50 p.m., Waisman later recalled, "I saw soldiers coming through the gate," among them Bass. "I took a look at his face and it was engraved on my memory."[48] Many years after the war's end,

Waisman searched for and found Bass and told him how much he meant to him. The two became friends and remained close until Bass's passing in 2015.

Burned into Humanity's Memory

Beyond the numerous personal stories from the Nazi camps loom the overarching horrors of those facilities forever burned into the historical memory of humanity as a whole. Decent people in each succeeding generation have agreed that the world must never forget what happened in those hellholes. This is why the Polish government turned the ruins of the remaining death camps into museums and memorials to the dead. These grim places, says Yitzhak Arad, "bear witness to the tragedies and massacres that were carried out on these sites and will remain for generations a mark of shame and disgrace, a reminder of the brutality and inhumanity that were the essence of Nazi Germany, and a warning to all peoples of the dangers of racism and hatred."[49]

SOURCE NOTES

Introduction: A Place of Life and Death

1. Erin Blakemore, "This Midwife at Auschwitz Delivered 3,000 Babies in Unfathomable Conditions," History, August 2, 2023. www.history.com.
2. Quoted in Meg Hunter-Kilmer, "Servant of God Stanisława Leszczyńska: The Midwife of Auschwitz Who Delivered Thousands of Babies and Saved Thousands of Lives," *Church Life Journal*, June 21, 2023. https://churchlifejournal.nd.edu.
3. Quoted in Blakemore, "This Midwife at Auschwitz Delivered 3,000 Babies in Unfathomable Conditions."
4. Nikolaus Wachsmann, *KL: A History of the Nazi Concentration Camps*. New York: Farrar, Straus, and Giroux, 2015, pp. 5–6.

Chapter One: Rise of the Nazi Death Camps

5. Quoted in Holocaust Historical Society, "Treblinka Eyewitness Statements," November 10, 2020. www.holocausthistorical society.org.uk.
6. Quoted in Holocaust Historical Society, "Treblinka Eyewitness Statements."
7. Quoted in Claudia Koonz, *Mothers in the Fatherland*. New York: St. Martin's, 1987, pp. 152–53.
8. Quoted in National World War II Museum, "The Exterminationist Mindset: Heinrich Himmler's October 1943 Speeches," October 23, 2023. www.nationalww2museum.org.
9. US Holocaust Memorial Museum, "'The Final Solution': Overview," December 8, 2020. https://encyclopedia.ushmm.org.
10. Quoted in Daniel Mendelsohn, *The Lost*. New York: HarperCollins, 2006, pp. 236–37.
11. Quoted in Holocaust Research Project, "Auschwitz Remembered," 2012. www.holocaustresearchproject.org.

Chapter Two: The Barest Existence

12. Quoted in Zidzislaw J. Ryn and Stanisław Kłodziński, "Hunger in the Concentration Camps, Part 1," *Medical Review Auschwitz*, November 8, 2022. www.mp.pl.
13. Quoted in Ryn and Kłodziński, "Hunger in the Concentration Camps, Part 1."

14. Quoted in Yitzhak Arad, *Belzec, Sobibor, Treblinka: The Operation Reinhard Death Camps*. Bloomington: University of Indiana Press, 1987, pp. 203–4.
15. Holocaust Research Project, "Majdanek Concentration Camp: Reception, Prisoners Daily Life, Sub-camps," 2007. www.holocaust researchproject.org.
16. Eve N. Soumerai and Carol D. Schulz, *Daily Life During the Holocaust*. Westport, CT: Greenwood, 2009, p. 185.
17. Quoted in Tiergartenstrasse 4 Association, "KL Bergen-Belsen." www.tiergartenstrasse4.org.
18. Quoted in South Carolina Council on the Holocaust, "Interview with Pincus Kolender." https://scholocaustcouncil.org.
19. Quoted in Bergen-Belsen.co.uk, "War Crimes Trials, Vol. II: The Belsen Trial. 'The Trial of Josef Kramer and Forty Four Others.'" www.bergenbelsen.co.uk.
20. Quoted in Bergen-Belsen.co.uk, "War Crimes Trials, Vol. II."
21. Soumerai and Schulz, *Daily Life During the Holocaust*, p. 103.
22. Gillian Brockell, "The First Transport of Jews to Auschwitz Was 997 Teenage Girls. Few Survived," *Washington Post*, January 27, 2020. www.washingtonpost.com.
23. Quoted in Kate Connolly, "'I Will Never Be Free of It': Auschwitz Survivor Recalls Horror 75 Years On," *The Guardian* (Manchester, UK), March 25, 2017. www.theguardian.com.

Chapter Three: Processing Death

24. Quoted in Mary Zobel, "Arriving at the Death Factory," Journey Through the Holocaust, 2024. https://journeythroughtheholocaust .org.
25. Quoted in Zobel, "Arriving at the Death Factory."
26. Quoted in Dirkdeklein, "Testimony of Barbara Stimler, Holocaust Survivor," *History of Sorts* (blog), July 7, 2022. https://dirkdeklein .net.
27. Quoted in US Holocaust Memorial Museum, "Oral History: Lilly Appelbaum Malnik Describes the Process of Registration at Auschwitz." www.ushmm.org.
28. Quoted in US Holocaust Memorial Museum, "Oral History: Hana Mueller Bruml Describes Arrival Procedures at Auschwitz." www .ushmm.org.
29. Quoted in Holocaust Research Project, "Auschwitz Remembered."
30. Quoted in Shirer, *The Rise and Fall of the Third Reich*, p. 968.

31. Quoted in Holocaust Historical Society, "Eyewitness Accounts of Round-ups and Mass Murders." www.holocausthistoricalsociety.org.uk.

Chapter Four: Resistance and Rebellion

32. Quoted in Jewish Virtual Library, "Escapee from Chelmno Documents Atrocities." www.jewishvirtuallibrary.org.
33. Arad, *Belzec, Sobibor, Treblinka*, pp. 282–83.
34. Jason Dawsey, "Remembering the Sobibor Uprising," National World War II Museum, November 14, 2018. www.nationalww2museum.org.
35. Quoted in Arad, *Belzec, Sobibor, Treblinka*, p. 327.
36. Quoted in Dawsey, "Remembering the Sobibor Uprising."
37. Dawsey, "Remembering the Sobibor Uprising."

Chapter Five: Downfall of the Camps and Liberation

38. Quoted in Facing History and Ourselves, "Eyewitness to Buchenwald," August 13, 2015. www.facinghistory.org.
39. Quoted in Facing History and Ourselves, "Eyewitness to Buchenwald."
40. Quoted in Facing History and Ourselves, "As the War Ended," August 2, 2016. www.facinghistory.org.
41. Quoted in Facing History and Ourselves, "As the War Ended."
42. Quoted in Saul Friedlander, *The Years of Extermination: Nazi Germany and the Jews, 1939–1945*. New York: HarperCollins, 2007, p. 648.
43. Louis L. Snyder, *The War: A Concise History, 1939–1945*. New York: Julian Messner, 1961, p. 423.
44. Quoted in Jewish Virtual Library, "Buchenwald: Report from Edward R. Murrow." www.jewishvirtuallibrary.org.
45. Quoted in USC Shoah Foundation, "Stories of Liberation," 2024. https://sfi.usc.edu.
46. Quoted in USC Shoah Foundation, "Stories of Liberation."
47. Quoted in Michel Martin, "WWII Veteran Remembers War, Discovers Truth," *Tell Me More*, NPR, November 27, 2008. www.npr.org.
48. Quoted in USC Shoah Foundation, "Stories of Liberation."
49. Arad, *Belzec, Sobibor, Treblinka*, p. 380.

Books

Nick Altman, *My Grandfather: The Last Nazi Death Camp Prisoner*. Self-published, Amazon Digital Services, 2023. Kindle.

Frank W. Baker, *We Survived the Holocaust: The Bluma and Felix Goldberg Story*. Irvington, NY: Imagine and Wonder, 2020.

Eva Mozes Kor, *Surviving the Angel of Death: The True Story of a Mengele Twin in Auschwitz*. Vancouver, BC: Tanglewood, 2020.

Nicola Pittam, *The Rebel Pianist of Majdanek: A Holocaust Story of Music and Survival in a Nazi Death Camp*. London: Mardle, 2024.

Winston Ramsey, *The Nazi Death Camps: Then and Now*. Riverside, CT: After the Battle, 2022.

Neal Shusterman, *Courage to Dream: Tales of Hope in the Holocaust*. New York: Graphix, 2023.

Internet Sources

Jason Dawsey, "Remembering the Sobibor Uprising," National World War II Museum November 14, 2018. www.nationalww2museum.org.

Facing History and Ourselves, "Eyewitness to Buchenwald," August 13, 2015. www.facinghistory.org.

Natasha Frost, "Horrors of Auschwitz: The Numbers Behind WWII's Deadliest Concentration Camp," History, July 13, 2023. www.history.com.

History, "Adolf Hitler," June 29, 2023. www.history.com.

Holocaust Historical Society, "Treblinka Eyewitness Statements," November 10, 2020. www.holocausthistoricalsociety.org.uk.

PBS, "Heinrich Himmler (1900–1945)." www.pbs.org.

Dave Roos, "The Horrifying Discovery of Dachau Concentration Camp—and Its Liberation by US Troops," History, August 3, 2023. www.history.com.

Jennifer Rosenberg, "Concentration and Death Camps Chart," Thought Co., March 23, 2020. http://history1900s.about.com.

South Carolina Council on the Holocaust, "Interview with Pincus Kolender." https://scholocaustcouncil.org.

Mary Zobel, "Arriving at the Death Factory," Journey Through the Holocaust, 2024. https://journeythroughtheholocaust.org.

Websites

Benjamin Describes Arriving at Auschwitz, PBS
www.pbs.org/video/benjamin-describes-arriving-auschwitz-6nczfr
This site contains a video in which a Polish Jew named Benjamin Lesser recalls his initial arrival at Auschwitz. Various links lead to more of his recollections of that infamous death camp.

Holocaust Survivors
www.holocaustsurvivors.org
This site contains an engrossing collection of personal narratives and recollections by several individuals who survived the Nazi death camps. Each narrative is accompanied by a photo of the survivor.

Jewish Virtual Library
www.jewishvirtuallibrary.org
The Jewish Virtual Library is an online research tool for topics that pertain to Judaism, Israel, and the Holocaust. The site features extensive primary source material, general information, and in-depth articles about all aspects of the Holocaust, including the Nazi death camps.

National World War II Museum
www.nationalww2museum.org
The National WWII Museum contains many exhibits, multimedia experiences, and a large collection of artifacts relating to that massive conflict. The website presents dozens of articles featuring detailed information about various aspects of the war.

Nazi Germany, Alpha History
https://alphahistory.com/nazigermany
This easy-to-read overview of the rise of the Third Reich contains numerous links to supplementary articles, including ones about Hitler, German militarism, the concentration camps, and key documents of the Nazi regime.

US Holocaust Memorial Museum
www.ushmm.org
This thoughtful and highly useful site contains numerous links to various aspects of Nazi Germany, the death camps, and the mass murders of Jews and others by the Nazis.

INDEX